THE AMERICAN GRILL

BY David Barich & Thomas Ingalls

PHOTOGRAPHY BY Dennis Bettencourt

FOOD STYLING BY Érez

SMITHMARK

This edition published in 1998 by
SMITHMARK Publishers
a division of U.S. Media Holdings, Inc.
115 West 18th Street, New York, NY 10011

SMITHMARK books are available for bulk purchase for sales promotion and premium use.
For details write or call the manager of special sales:
SMITHMARK Publishers
115 West 18th Street
New York, NY 10011
(212) 519-1300

The American Grill was produced by
David Barich & Associates
870 Market Street, Suite 690
San Francisco, CA 94102
(45) 288-4525
Email dbarich@barichbooks.com

Printed and bound in Singapore

Library of Congress Catalog Card Number: 97-62208

ISBN 0-7651-9076-1

Produced by David Barich

Jacket Cover Design: Melanie Random
Interior Book Design: Ingalls + Associates
Designers: Tom Ingalls, Tracy Dean, and Margot Scaccabarrozzi
Photography by Dennis Bettencourt
Photographer's Assistant: Jean Lannen
Food and Prop Styling by Érez

"Grilling, broiling, barbecuing — whatever you want to call it — is an art, not just a matter of building a pyre and throwing on a piece of meat as a sacrifice to the gods of the stomach."

— James Beard, *Beard on Food*

CONTENTS

Introduction

Americans love to grill. From city and suburban cookouts to weekend outings in the country and tailgate picnics in football stadium parking lots, the fragrance of charcoal is part of the American atmosphere. The grill has been popular in this country's cuisine—and a fixture in its backyards—since the fifties, when the first built-in barbecues and portable grills became part of the middle-class package of a house in the suburbs and a two-car garage. But the grill goes back much farther than that in our history—in fact, it predates the country of the United States itself. The first record of a grill on this continent was noted by the Spanish, who found the "Indians" of the Caribbean using a woven grid of green wood to suspend food over a fire. The Spanish version of the Native American name for this device—*barbacoa*—would eventually be used to describe a unique and varied subculture of American cuisine: the pit barbecues of the American South and West.

Today the word *barbecue* is used to describe almost anything cooked outdoors on a grill, and it is also used to refer to the grill itself as well as to the act of grilling. We like to use the word as it first evolved in America: to refer to food that has been cooked over low heat for a relatively long time and that is basted or served—sometimes both—with a spicy, intensely flavored sauce.

This method of cooking was perfected in the southern part of the United States and in Mexico, where feasts were centered on the cooking of whole pigs or calves in closed or open pits. In either case, the sauces that were concocted to be served with the cooked meat were also cooked for a long time, and their varied ingredients reflected a mixed heritage of African, Spanish, Native American, and Mexican influences: many spices and herbs, tomatoes and chilies, mustard, sometimes vinegar, sugar, onions, garlic. The barbecue became the focal point of community celebrations and civic gatherings all over the United States and was an integral part of the cattle runs of the Old West.

From the pit barbecue to the cowboy campfire, cooking fires were almost always fueled by wood, so abundant in many parts of the country. But in 1924, one of the greatest of American entrepreneurs, Henry Ford, set the stage for charcoal cookery as we know it today. The body of the Model T was made using hardwood from Wisconsin, and when leftover wood scrap accumulated at Ford's factory there, he built a charcoal plant and developed the briquette. Because there were more briquettes than American industry could use, Ford decided to market them to the public for cooking out of doors, using his own Ford dealers as distributors. The briquette plant was eventually acquired by the Kingsford Company, and soon charcoal briquettes were available at grocery and hardware stores all over the country.

The American grill pantry is much larger now than in those early days. It holds not only such classic prepared condiments as Worcestershire sauce and Tabasco sauce but newer ingredients such as balsamic vinegar and tomatillos as well. American cuisine has expanded to include foods from all around the world, reflecting both the amazing mixture of peoples that make up this country as well as a new fascination with food and cooking that embraces new dishes and flavors with enthusiasm. Our chapter on American ingredients discusses some of the classic and newly adopted favorites used in recipes in this book.

The twelve menus in *The American Grill* are organized by region, from the north country of wild ducks and wild rice to the Tex-Mex and Hispanic-Latino influences of the Southwest, from the Southern barbecue of Memphis,

Tennessee, to the Mediterranean-influenced cuisine of California, and encompassing the European-derived recipes of the Midwest and Northeast, such as wilted salad, coleslaw, potato salad, and marinated cucumber and onion salad. The ingredients include such indigenous American foods as turkey, salmon, chilies, tomatoes, sweet potatoes, potatoes, and corn, all presented in simple grilled main dishes and in side dishes that are either grilled or prepared in the kitchen. Each menu includes two side dishes, with suggestions for a third (often one from another menu) and for appropriate beverages to accompany the food. Although most of the recipes are simple, the grilling instructions are detailed. All recipes were tested using mesquite charcoal and a kettle grill with the cooking rack fixed 6 inches from the fuel grate.

In the last few years, grilling has become even more popular in America, and grill cuisine has become more sophisticated. The grilled foods of many other cuisines are found in American backyards and restaurants. Outdoor menus are no longer limited to hamburgers and hot dogs, and grill equipment has become more specialized. Today the grill cook can choose from an entire *batterie* of grill tools, smoking woods, hardwood charcoals, and grill accessories. Our chapter on basic grilling will help to demystify the process and guide you in choosing the tools you will use the most.

In *The American Grill* we've tried to combine the best of the traditional grilled foods of the past with the best of the newer foods of today. It's a combination of recipes inspired by the heritage of cowboys and Native Americans, trappers and sheepherders, immigrant cooks from all over the world, and contemporary American chefs. Whether you set up your grill in the countryside, on a city balcony, or in your own backyard, we hope this little book will find a place nearby.

INGREDIENTS & TECHNIQUES

AMERICAN INGREDIENTS

Buttermilk: A characteristic ingredient of American baked goods, buttermilk adds its tangy taste to a variety of foods and is a good low-fat substitute for cream in many recipes. If you don't have buttermilk on hand, make your own soured milk substitute by adding 1 tablespoon fresh lemon juice or distilled white vinegar to 1 cup milk; let stand for 5 minutes.

Cheeses: The United States produces many excellent cheeses, but the best **Gruyère** and **Parmesan** are still made in France and Italy, respectively. Although these cheeses are expensive, their superior taste makes them worth the extra cost.

Chilies: Native to North America and now developing a cult following in this country, the many kinds of chilies may be divided into those that are fresh and those that are dried. This book uses fresh **jalapeños,** which are small, tapered green chilies that turn red when ripened, and poblanos, larger black-green triangular-shaped chilies. Jalapeños are widely available; **serranos,** which are similar to jalapeños in appearance but slightly hotter, may be substituted. Poblanos are available in many produce stores, especially Latino markets; **bell peppers, green Anaheims,** or **New Mexico chilies** may be substituted, but none of them have the deep, complex smoky-hot taste of the poblano. **Canned peeled green chilies** add a mild heat to many Tex-Mex dishes. Dried chilies are found in this book in the form of **paprika, cayenne** (which we love for the vibrancy only the smallest amount can add to a dish), and **dried red pepper flakes.** The last two and Tabasco sauce are interchangeable in many dishes.

Corn: This American grain in its many different forms is a natural with grilled foods. Try to get the freshest organic corn you can find for recipes using fresh corn.

Organic stone-ground cornmeal is the best product for baking.

Fish and shellfish: Buy clean-smelling and bright-looking fish from a reputable fishmonger to make sure the quality is high. For the freshest cuts, ask to have chunks and fillets custom cut from the whole fish, if possible. Cook fish within 24 hours of purchase, and make sure the cooking rack is clean and oiled so that the fish won't tear when you turn it.

Herbs: In marinades, dry rubs, and cooked sauces, you may substitute dried crushed thyme, rosemary, sage, and oregano in a 1 to 3 ratio for fresh herbs. Parsley and basil, however, lose so much flavor in the drying process that they should always be used only in fresh form. Flat-leaf, or Italian, parsley is superior in flavor to curly-leaf parsley.

Meats: Look for naturally raised beef, ham, lamb, and veal. They have less fat, more taste, and no artificial hormones. To be absolutely sure that all bacteria have been killed by the cooking process, meat must be cooked medium-well done, or to a temperature of 160°F. If you prefer the better taste and texture of less-well-done meat, buy it from a trusted specialty butcher; this goes a long way toward ensuring high quality and cleanliness.

Oils: Canola oil is lowest in saturated fats of all oils and has a fairly high burning point; use it when you want a mild-tasting oil. **Corn oil** and **olive oil** are both used in Mexican and Southwestern cooking, and olive oil, along with many other Italian foodstuffs, has been thoroughly integrated into American cuisine. Use regular, mild-tasting olive oil in all recipes except for some salad dressings in which the strong, fruity taste of extra-virgin olive oil is desirable. Corn oil is good for deep-frying and for whenever you are cooking with corn in any other form.

Poultry: Naturally raised chicken, turkey, and duck are slightly more expensive than other poultry, but because they are lower in fat and higher in tenderness and taste, they are worth it. Naturally raised birds were used in this book; the cooking times for pen-raised hormone-fed birds may be slightly longer. Poultry is considered absolutely safe to eat when it reaches an internal temperature of 170°F in the breast

meat and 180°F in a thigh, although many people prefer it less well done.

Smoking woods: Vine cuttings and a variety of fragrant wood chips add depth and complexity to grilled foods. Hickory is traditional for many Southern foods, mesquite is used particularly in the Southwest, apple or alder is good with salmon and other fish, and olive wood and vine cuttings go well with Mediterranean-inspired dishes.

Tabasco sauce: Produced on Avery Island, Louisiana, by the McIlhenny family since 1868, Tabasco sauce adds its fiery taste to foods from Bloody Marys to taco sauce. It may be used in place of cayenne pepper or dried red pepper flakes.

Tomatoes: Try to find vine-ripened organic tomatoes—they do exist, in natural foods stores, farmer's markets, and outdoor farm stands. If you can't get good regular tomatoes, use cherry tomatoes, which usually have an excellent flavor.

Tomatillos: Available fresh in some supermarkets and in Latino markets, these pale green husk tomatoes are also widely available in cans.

Vinegars: Distilled white vinegar is a clear, clean-tasting condiment that may be interchanged with rice wine vinegar. A good balsamic vinegar will transform salad greens and vegetables with its sweet, aged flavor. White wine vinegar and red wine vinegar are in between distilled and balsamic in their flavor range.

Wild rice: An indigenous grain that is now farmed, wild rice also still grows in the wild in Minnesota, Wisconsin, and Michigan, where it is hand-gathered by Native Americans. Although it is expensive, there is no real substitute for its nutty and woodsy flavor.

Worcestershire sauce: Although English in origin, this pungent condiment has been completely assimilated into American cuisine and is a classic ingredient in barbecue sauces.

BASIC GRILLING

Grilling can seem complicated or daunting because people are not used to cooking with a fuel source that isn't regulated by a button or a dial. Yet it is the primal aspect of cooking over an elemental source of fire that yields much of the pleasure of grilling. The more you grill the easier it becomes, of course; a few basic pointers will do a lot to help you along the way.

1. Keep the Cooking Rack Clean: It's important to periodically clean the ashes out of the bottom of your grill (although ashes also help to insulate and keep temperatures even), but it's much more important to keep the cooking rack clean. Not only will a build-up of old food and cooking juices give your latest grill effort an off taste, delicate foods such as fish will stick to a dirty grill. A wire grill brush (see page 25) is invaluable for cleaning the cooking rack quickly and efficiently. Use it after each grill meal. If you've forgotten, use the grill brush before you grill next time, especially when you will be grilling fish.

2. Use Hardwood Charcoal: The easiest way to ensure good grilling is to use natural charcoal made from mesquite or other kinds of hardwood, not briquettes. Briquettes are made with fillers and are chemically treated, and they inevitably add an off taste to grilled food, while hardwood charcoal gives food the slight perfume of the wood from which it was made. Briquettes also burn at a lower heat than does natural charcoal, yet they burn up faster because of their fillers. Hardwood charcoal is thus more economical, despite its higher initial cost.

Mesquite is the hardwood charcoal of choice, both for its distinctive fragrance and because it burns hotter than other hardwoods, allowing you to sear foods

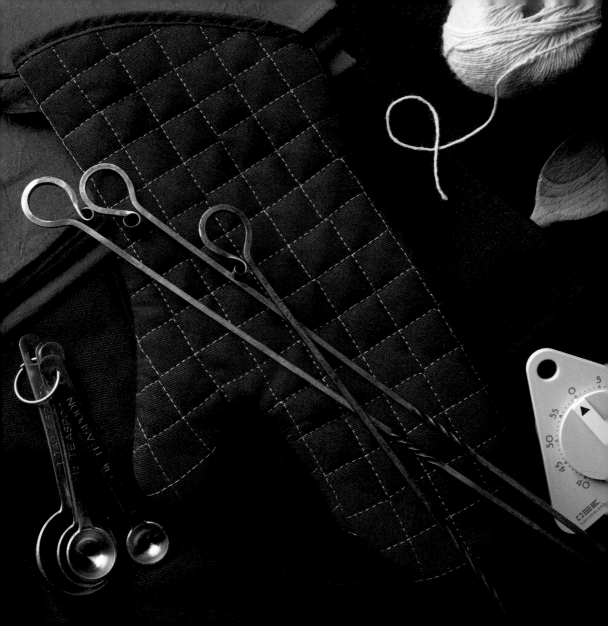

more efficiently. Mesquite does take getting used to, though: It sometimes comes in large hunks that need to be broken up with a hammer or an axe, and it shoots off an alarming number of sparks when it's first lighted—you will need to make sure your grill isn't near anything flammable, including you and your clothes. The other problem with mesquite is that it isn't as available as briquettes, although this is changing. If you love to grill, look in our mail-order section on pages 68–69, order mesquite in quantity, and keep it in a large waterproof plastic garbage can near your grill.

3. Use a Charcoal Chimney: Don't use charcoal lighter to start your grill fire. It's cheaper and more reliable to use a charcoal chimney, and the chemical taste of charcoal lighter is not imparted to the food (or its chemical wastes to the air we breathe). To use this large metal canister with a handle on one side, place a sheet or two of wadded-up newspaper in the bottom and pile small chunks of hardwood charcoal on top. Take the cooking grate off the grill and place the chimney in the center of the fuel grate. Light the newspaper and let the

chimney sit until the coals are lighted. Empty the lighted coals into the fuel grate and cover them with the desired amount of charcoal for whatever you're grilling. The new charcoal will quickly light on fire. Allow 30 to 45 minutes from the time you light the coals in the charcoal chimney to the time the fire is ready for grilling.

4. Know When to Use a Direct or an Indirect Fire: A direct fire is just what it sounds like: The food to be cooked is placed on the cooking rack directly above the lighted coals. Such a fire is used for foods that cook relatively quickly, usually anything that is thinner than 1½ inches or so. Foods that cook very quickly, such as ground meats and thinly sliced pieces of meat or vegetables, are cooked entirely over a direct fire on an open grill. Foods that take a little longer to cook, such as thick steaks and chops or pieces of chicken, are usually seared on all sides over a direct fire, after which the grill is covered to allow the food to cook more evenly.

An indirect fire is used for thicker pieces of food, such as roasts and whole fish. In this case, the lighted coals are formed into a circle or two banks, and a metal drip pan is placed in the center. We like to use two banks of coals propped up with metal charcoal rails, because more coals can be stacked up and the fire is in less danger of dying. The indirect heat cooks food more slowly and evenly, while the drip pan catches the fat and drippings from the grilling food. If the food isn't too fatty, the drip pan may be used to cook foods such as potatoes and other root vegetables. Or, you may add water or flavoring liquids to the drip pan to mingle with the drippings (and to help keep the grilling food moist). Degreased and reduced if necessary, this liquid makes an excellent sauce.

5. Use the Right Amount of Coals:
It's better to use too many coals than too few. For a direct fire, the charcoal when spread out in one layer should cover an area slightly larger in diameter than the food itself. For an indirect fire, use about twice as many coals; they will be pushed into banks or a circle and will need to burn for a longer time.

6. Learn to Judge the Heat of the Fire:
The fire is *hot* when the coals are red but covered with a layer of white ash; at this heat you will be able to hold your hand 6 inches from the cooking rack for 3 to 4 seconds. This heat is right for most foods to be cooked directly over the coals. The fire is *medium hot* when you can barely see the red coals glowing through the ashes, and you can hold your hand 6 inches from the cooking rack for 5 to 7 seconds. This stage is used for indirect fires and covered grilling. The fire is *low* when the coals are completely gray. This is the stage the fire eventually will slow to when the grill is covered.

7. Learn to Use Smoking Woods:
To add the flavor of aromatic wood smoke to your food, soak wood chips or vine cuttings in water to cover for 30 minutes to 1 hour. Drain them, then sprinkle them evenly over the coals. Cover the grill, partially close the vents, and cook the food until done.

8. Learn to Regulate the Fire:
To make a fire burn hotter, you can do one or more of the following things: (1) Knock

accumulated ashes off the coals by shaking the grill or tapping the coals with a metal tool such as a pair of tongs; (2) push the coals closer together; (3) completely open the top and bottom grill vents (on the lid and on the bottom of the grill). If the coals are used up, you will have to rebuild the fire by adding new coals (see below). *To make a fire burn more slowly,* you can (1) put the lid on the grill; (2) partially close the grill vents; (3) push the coals farther apart. To put out flare-ups, cover the grill. If this doesn't work, as a last resort, spray the fire with water (see page 25).

9. Learn How to Rebuild the Fire:

If you haven't used enough coals to start with, or if you've been cooking for an hour or longer, you will need to rebuild the fire. The easiest way to do this is to light a charcoal chimney full of coals about 10 minutes before you want to use them to rebuild your fire. (Be sure to put the chimney on a fireproof surface, such as the fuel bed of a small portable grill.) Otherwise you will have to add unlighted coals to the coals in the grill and wait 10 to 20 minutes until they are ready to use.

10. Learn to Tell When Food Is Cooked:

There are several ways to tell when food is done. We've tried to give you exact times, but there are so many variables in grilling that you will need to learn doneness signs for yourself. Appearances can be deceiving; if your fire is too hot, the outside of food will be charred while the inside is still raw. Experienced cooks can tell doneness by touch: If a piece of meat or chicken is soft, it is rare; if slightly resistant, it is medium; and if stiff, well done. An instant-read thermometer is a great help, but it works only in pieces of food that are at least 2 inches thick. Pieces of steak, chicken breasts, fish, and vegetables may have to be cut into to see whether they are sufficiently cooked. Large pieces of food such as roasts and whole birds will begin to shrink slightly when they are done; when a piece of poultry is pierced with a knife, the juices should run clear.

GRILL TOOLS

Along with a sturdy grill, you will need the following tools in order to grill safely and well.

Charcoal chimney: Use this device instead of charcoal lighter.

Instant-read thermometer: A few minutes before you think meat or chicken might be done, insert this kind of thermometer to check the internal temperature.

Spray bottle: Keep a bottle of water with a spray attachment by the grill at all times. You can dampen most flares by covering the grill, but you should have water ready in case this doesn't work.

Long-handled tongs: Save yourself trouble and burns by using a pair of metal tongs with spoon-shaped ends. Available in restaurant supply stores, these inexpensive tongs can be used to stir and move coals, to scoop basting liquid, and to turn almost anything on the grill. Store the tongs by hanging them over the grill's wooden handle.

Timer: Always use a timer when grilling; it's easy to become distracted, especially when you're cooking for a group. Look for the kind that clips onto your apron.

Wire grill brush: This metal-bristled brush is essential for keeping the cooking rack clean. Use it after each grill session.

Other good grill tools include *grill mitts,* a *long-handled basting brush,* a *long-handled bent-blade spatula, charcoal rails* (to hold up banks of coals for an indirect fire), and *grill baskets* and *grilling grids* (small-meshed or perforated metal containers useful for small pieces of food, such as sliced vegetables or fish fillets, that otherwise would fall through the cooking rack). All of these tools are available at good kitchenware and hardware stores, or see Mail-Order Sources, pages 68–69.

AMERICAN GRILL MENUS

TEXAS BARBECUED RIBS

Red and Green Coleslaw • Skillet Corn Bread with Green Chilies

Serves 4 to 6

This is a good menu to multiply for a large group. The potato salad on page 42 would be a nice addition, and beer, lemonade, and iced tea all go well with these dishes.

Texas Barbecued Ribs

4 pounds beef spareribs, or 1 slab pork
  spareribs
Olive oil for coating
Salt and freshly ground black pepper
  to taste

SAUCE

3 tablespoons butter
1 onion, chopped
4 garlic cloves, minced
2 tomatoes, chopped
One 6-ounce can tomato paste
¼ teaspoon Tabasco sauce
1 teaspoon Worcestershire sauce
½ cup brown sugar
1 tablespoon Dijon mustard
Dash of paprika

Salt to taste
Cayenne pepper to taste
½ cup dry red wine
Juice of 1 lemon

Prepare an indirect charcoal fire in a grill. Rub the spareribs all over with olive oil and sprinkle on both sides with salt and pepper. Set aside at room temperature.

To make the sauce: In a large sauté pan or skillet, heat the butter until it bubbles. Add the onion and garlic and sauté until translucent, about 3 minutes. Add all of the remaining ingredients, stir to blend, and cook over medium-low heat for 20 to 30 minutes, or until the mixture is slightly thickened and the flavors have ripened. Adjust the seasoning.

When the coals are medium hot, place the ribs fat-side down in the center of the cooking rack. Cover the grill, partially open the vents, and cook the ribs for 1 hour, turning them every 15 minutes.

After 1 hour, rebuild the fire by adding more coals. Baste the ribs evenly on both sides with the sauce and cook another 30 minutes, turning and basting on both sides every 10 minutes, for a total cooking time of 1½ hours. The meat should be just barely pale pink.

Skillet Corn Bread with Green Chilies

1 cup unbleached all-purpose flour
1 cup cornmeal
1 tablespoon sugar
1 teaspoon salt
2 teaspoons baking powder
1 teaspoon baking soda
2 eggs
1¼ cups buttermilk
2 tablespoons butter, melted, plus
   2 teaspoons unmelted butter
2 tablespoons canola or corn oil
1 cup fresh or thawed frozen corn
   kernels
¼ cup canned peeled green chilies,
   drained and minced

Preheat the oven to 400°F. In a large bowl, mix together the flour, cornmeal, sugar, salt, baking powder, and baking soda. In a medium bowl, beat the eggs. Mix in the buttermilk, melted butter, and oil. Add the liquid ingredients to the dry ingredients and stir until just combined. Stir in the corn kernels and chilies.

In an 8-inch cast-iron skillet or an 8-inch square baking pan, melt the 2 teaspoons butter and tilt the pan to coat the bottom and sides. Pour in the corn bread batter and bake for 25 minutes, or until the top is golden brown and set.

Red and Green Coleslaw

3 cups shredded red cabbage
3 cups shredded green cabbage
1 small red onion, cut into thin slices
2 tablespoons olive oil
2 tablespoons red wine vinegar
½ cup minced fresh cilantro
½ teaspoon salt, or to taste
1 teaspoon sugar, or to taste
⅛ teaspoon cayenne pepper, or to taste

In a large ceramic or glass bowl, combine the cabbage, onion, oil, and vinegar; toss to mix. Stir in the remaining ingredients and correct the seasoning. Let sit at room temperature for 30 minutes, or cover and refrigerate for 1 hour.

GRILL-ROASTED WHOLE TURKEY

Waldorf Salad • Green Rice Casserole

Serves 8 to 10

Turkey is great for summer grilling. Here it's accompanied with two classic American dishes, Waldorf salad and green rice casserole. For a vegetable, try grilled sweet potatoes or grilled tomatoes. To drink: Zinfandel or Chardonnay.

Grill-roasted Whole Turkey

One fresh 10 to 12-pound turkey
2 cups dry white wine
2 cups water
Salt and freshly ground pepper
1 orange, cut into eighths
1 onion, cut into eighths
4 *each* fresh thyme and marjoram sprigs
2 celery stalks with leaves
2 tablespoons olive oil

Build an indirect charcoal fire in a grill and place a 9-by-13-inch metal drip pan in the center of the fuel grate. Add the wine and water to the drip pan. Rinse the turkey inside and out and dry it with paper towels. Sprinkle the inside of the bird with salt and pepper and stuff it with the orange, onion, thyme, marjoram, and celery. Truss the turkey and rub it with olive oil. Let sit at room temperature until the fire is ready.

When the coals are medium hot, place the turkey breast-side up in the center of the grill. Partially close the vents and cook the turkey for 3½ hours. The internal temperature of the grill should remain at around 350°F. Rebuild the fire by adding more coals after each hour of cooking; add more water to the drip pan if necessary. When the breast meat registers 165°F, transfer the turkey from the grill to a platter and cover it loosely with aluminum foil; let sit for 15 minutes. Meanwhile, degrease the liquid in the dripping pan. Uncover, carve, and serve the turkey with the pan juice alongside.

Green Rice Casserole

5 cups water
2 teaspoons salt, or to taste
2½ cups rice
2 eggs, beaten
3 cups milk
1 cup *each* minced fresh parsley and
  spinach
3 garlic cloves, minced
2 cups shredded Monterey jack cheese
1¼ cups finely shredded Parmesan
  cheese
1 teaspoon curry powder
2 teaspoons olive oil

In a large saucepan, bring the water and
1 teaspoon of the salt to a boil. Stir the
rice into the water, reduce heat, cover, and
simmer for about 25 to 30 minutes. Fluff
the rice with a fork and cook uncovered
for 2 or 3 minutes; set aside.

Preheat the oven to 325°F. Butter a
12-cup casserole or baking dish or pan.
In a large bowl, combine the rice, eggs,
milk, parsley, spinach, garlic, 1½ cups of
the Monterey jack, 1 cup of the Parmesan,
and curry powder; mix thoroughly. Pour
into the prepared dish or pan. Mix the
remaining ½ cup Monterey jack and
¼ cup Parmesan and sprinkle it evenly

over the top. Drizzle the olive oil over the
cheese. Bake for about 30 minutes, or
until lightly browned. Serve warm.

Waldorf Salad

8 Pippin or other tart, firm apples,
  peeled, cored, and diced
8 celery sticks, cut into small dice
1½ cups seedless grapes, halved
1 cup golden raisins
¼ cup minced green onions
1½ cups walnuts
¾ cup mayonnaise
½ cup plain yogurt
2 tablespoons honey
Juice of 1 lemon, or to taste
Salt, freshly ground white pepper,
  paprika, and ground cinnamon to taste

In a large nonaluminum bowl, combine
the apples, celery, grapes, raisins, green
onions, and walnuts. In a small bowl,
blend together the mayonnaise, yogurt,
honey, and lemon juice. Stir this mixture
into the apple mixture to coat thoroughly.
Add the remaining ingredients; stir to
blend. Cover and chill in the refrigerator.
Stir again before serving.

Cajun Shrimp

Hickory-smoked Tomatoes • Dirty Rice

Serves 4 to 6

The flavors of the Louisiana countryside: shrimp and tomatoes cooked on the grill, served with "dirty rice" speckled with minced giblets. Serve with your favorite cold beer.

Cajun Shrimp

2 pounds large shrimp (16 to 20 per pound), peeled

Cajun Spice Mix

¼ teaspoon cayenne pepper
2 teaspoons paprika
1 teaspoon dried thyme
½ teaspoon *each* freshly ground white pepper and dried red pepper flakes
1 teaspoon ground cumin

Juice of 1 lemon
¼ cup olive oil
4 garlic cloves, chopped
Lemon wedges for garnish

Light a charcoal fire in a grill. Using metal skewers, thread each shrimp through the head and tail so that the shrimp will lie flat on the grill. Place the skewers in a large nonaluminum baking dish or pan. Combine all the ingredients for the spice mix and sprinkle the mix evenly over both sides of the shrimp. In a small bowl, combine all of the remaining ingredients except the lemon wedges and pour them over the shrimp. Rub the spices and liquid into the shrimp; let sit at room temperature while the coals are heating.

When the coals are hot, place the skewers on the cooking rack and grill for 3 minutes on each side, or until the shrimp are evenly pink and opaque. Serve garnished with lemon wedges.

Dirty Rice

5 cups low-salt canned chicken broth
4 chicken gizzards
4 ounces chicken livers
8 ounces ground pork
2 tablespoons canola oil
1 small onion, finely chopped
1 red bell pepper, cored, seeded, and
 finely chopped
3 garlic cloves, minced
3 green onions, finely chopped
2½ cups rice
1 teaspoon salt
¼ teaspoon cayenne pepper
1 teaspoon *each* paprika and freshly
 ground white pepper

In a medium saucepan, heat the chicken broth to a simmer and add the gizzards. Cover the pan and cook the gizzards for 15 minutes; add the livers and cook for 5 minutes. Drain the gizzards and livers, reserving the broth. Let the gizzards and livers cool slightly, then chop them finely.

In a large skillet, cook the pork over medium-low heat, stirring, for 3 to 5 minutes, or until it is no longer pink. Remove the meat from the pan with a slotted spoon and pour out all the fat. Add the canola oil to the pan and heat over medium heat. Add the onion, pepper, garlic, and green onions to the pan and sauté for 3 minutes, or until the onion is translucent. Add the rice and chopped gizzards and livers, and cook and stir 3 to 5 minutes, or until the rice is opaque. Pour the reserved chicken broth into the skillet and add the remaining ingredients. Bring the mixture to a boil, then lower heat, cover, and simmer for 15 minutes, or until the rice is tender and has absorbed the broth. Place the skillet, uncovered, in a 250°F oven for 15 minutes; serve warm.

Hickory-smoked Tomatoes

Soak ½ cup hickory chips in water to cover for 30 minutes. Coat 1 basket of stemmed cherry tomatoes with olive oil and sprinkle with salt and pepper to taste. Drain the hickory chips and sprinkle them over medium-hot coals. Place the stemmed cherry tomatoes in a grill basket or on a grill rack, cover the grill, partially close the vents, and cook for 6 minutes. Transfer to a bowl and serve warm.

Northwest Salmon with Basil Butter

Grilled Corn on the Cob • Romaine Salad with Oregon Blue Cheese

Serves 6

No food is more evocative of the Pacific Northwest than salmon. Our menu combines this full-flavored fish with a bright green basil butter, which is also good spread on the grilled corn. A green salad with pungent Oregon blue cheese completes the meal, and a California Chardonnay is an ideal companion.

Northwest Salmon with Basil Butter

One 3-pound center-cut salmon chunk, or one 6-pound whole salmon
½ cup alder wood chips
¼ cup olive oil
Juice of 1 lemon
Salt and freshly ground white pepper to taste

Basil Butter

1 bunch basil, stemmed (reserve 4 sprigs for garnish)

1 tablespoon olive oil
2 tablespoons plain yogurt
½ cup unsalted whipped butter at room temperature
Salt and freshly ground white pepper to taste
1 teaspoon fresh lemon juice, or to taste

Prepare a charcoal fire in a grill and place the alder wood chips in water to cover. If you are using a whole fish, cut off the head and tail. Open the salmon and cut partially through the flesh down the center along one side of the backbone. Press the salmon open flat like a book. Pull out the backbone and the diagonal bones; you may need tweezers to remove all the diagonal bones. In a small bowl, combine the oil and lemon juice, and brush this mixture over the flesh side of the salmon; sprinkle with salt and pepper. Set the salmon aside at room temperature.

To make the basil butter: Place the basil, oil, and yogurt in a blender or food processor and blend until coarsely pureed. Add the butter and blend to a very smooth puree. Place the basil butter in a small bowl and add salt, pepper, and lemon juice. Adjust the seasoning and set aside at room temperature.

When the coals are hot, drain the alder wood chips and sprinkle them over the coals. Place the salmon skin-side down in the center of the grill, cover, and grill for 10 to 15 minutes without turning, or until the outside of the salmon is opaque but the center is still translucent (cook a few more minutes if you prefer salmon opaque throughout). With a long spatula or 2 regular spatulas, transfer the salmon from the grill to a warm serving plate or plates. Serve with a dollop of basil butter on top and the remainder alongside.

Grilled Corn on the Cob

Choose 6 plump ears of very fresh unhusked and untrimmed sweet corn. (Ideally, the corn should have been picked no more than 1 day ahead of cooking.) Place the ears of corn in a large container of cold water to cover and let soak for about 30 minutes. Drain the soaked ears and grill them unhusked on a cooking rack over hot coals, turning occasionally, for about 15 minutes. Let each guest husk his or her own ear of corn, and use a little of the basil butter as a sauce.

Romaine Salad with Oregon Blue Cheese

2 heads romaine lettuce
12 thin slices red onion
1 cup stemmed red, orange, or yellow cherry or baby plum tomatoes, or a mixture of colors
½ cup olive oil
3 tablespoons red wine vinegar
Salt and freshly ground white pepper to taste
½ cup crumbled Oregon or other blue cheese

Tear the romaine leaves into large pieces and place them in a salad bowl with the onion slices and tomatoes. In a small bowl, whisk the oil and vinegar together. Pour this mixture over the salad ingredients and toss to coat them. Add salt and pepper and toss again. Sprinkle on the blue cheese and toss to combine.

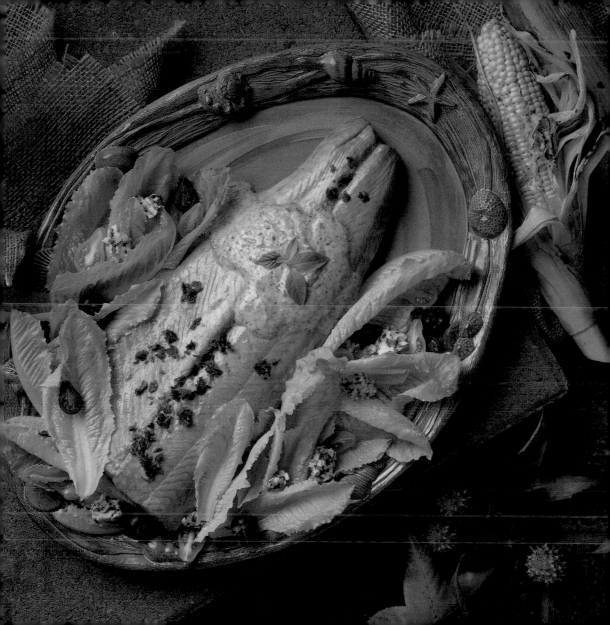

MEMPHIS BARBECUED CHICKEN

Wilted Salad • Midwest Potato Salad

Serves 4

In Memphis barbecue, a variety of dry spice rubs add flavor to grilled and pit-roasted meats. A spice rub is a quick way to give a barbecue taste to chicken, here cut into quarters for easy cooking and served with a wilted salad and a classic American potato salad. This is a good menu to multiply for a group. If you want to add a vegetable, try the grilled corn on page 38, served with the basil butter from the same menu. To drink: iced tea, lemonade, or beer.

Memphis Barbecued Chicken

One 3½-pound chicken, cut into quarters
Olive oil for coating
1 cup hickory chips (optional)

DRY SPICE RUB

1 teaspoon salt
2 teaspoons brown sugar
¼ teaspoon ground ginger
1 teaspoon dry mustard
¼ teaspoon cayenne pepper
⅛ teaspoon ground allspice
4 teaspoons sweet Hungarian paprika

Ask your butcher to cut the chicken into quarters, or cut it yourself by first halving it lengthwise, then cutting each half into a breast and wing quarter and a thigh and leg quarter. Place the chicken on a platter and coat it evenly all over with olive oil.

Prepare a charcoal fire in a grill and place the optional hickory chips in water to cover. To make the spice rub: In a small bowl, combine all the ingredients and blend thoroughly. Rub the spice mixture evenly over all sides of the quartered chicken and let sit at room temperature until the coals are ready.

When the coals are hot, sear the chicken on each side for 5 minutes. If using the hickory chips, drain them and sprinkle them over the coals. Partially open the vents, cover the grill, and cook the chicken another 10 minutes on each side, for a total cooking time of 30 minutes, or until the skin is brown and crisp and the juices run clear when the chicken is pierced with a knife. Remove the chicken from the grill, cover it with aluminum foil, and let sit for 10 minutes before serving.

Wilted Salad

½ bunch spinach, stemmed
1 bunch watercress, stemmed
1 head red leaf lettuce
½ sweet white onion, cut into thin
   slices
8 red radishes, cut into very thin slices
1 bacon strip
3 tablespoons olive oil
1 tablespoon distilled white vinegar
1 tablespoon red wine vinegar
½ teaspoon sugar
Salt and freshly ground white pepper
   to taste

Place the greens in a large glass, ceramic, or wooden bowl. Add the onion and

radish slices. In a small skillet, cook the bacon strip until crisp. Remove the bacon from the pan with a spatula and drain it well on a paper towel. Pour off all the bacon fat and set the skillet aside. Let the bacon cool slightly, then cut it into very small pieces; set aside.

Just before serving the salad, heat the olive oil in the skillet that was used to cook the bacon. When the oil is fragrant, stir in the vinegars and sugar. Pour the hot mixture over the greens, stirring them to coat and wilt the leaves. Add salt and pepper to taste. Sprinkle the chopped bacon over the salad and serve at once.

Midwest Potato Salad

1½ pounds unpeeled white or red
   boiling potatoes
2 eggs
4 tablespoons good-quality mayonnaise
2 tablespoons plain yogurt
2 teaspoons white wine vinegar
2 teaspoons Dijon mustard
¼ cup minced fresh flat-leaf parsley
¼ cup finely chopped red onion
½ teaspoon celery seed
Salt, paprika, and freshly ground white
   pepper to taste

Place the potatoes in a large saucepan and add salted water to cover. Cover the pan and bring the water to a boil. Reduce heat to a simmer and boil the potatoes until tender, about 45 minutes for large potatoes. Test for doneness by inserting a knife into the center of the potatoes, but don't test until well along in the cooking process, as too-frequent testing will make the potatoes fall apart. Drain the potatoes and place them on a plate in the refrigerator until completely cooled, 30 minutes or longer.

Meanwhile, place the eggs in a small saucepan of salted water to cover. Bring the water to a boil, reduce heat to low, and simmer the eggs for 10 minutes. With a slotted spoon, remove the eggs from the pan and place them in a bowl of cold water.

When the potatoes are completely cooled, peel them and cut them into ½-inch dice. Place the diced potatoes in a large ceramic, glass, or stainless steel bowl. Peel and chop the eggs; add them to the potatoes. In a small bowl, blend together all the remaining ingredients. Taste for seasoning. Pour this mixture over the potatoes and eggs; stir gently to coat. Correct the seasoning, stirring any additions into the salad gently to prevent the potatoes from falling apart. Cover and chill in the refrigerator until serving.

FILLET STEAKS WITH RED WINE

Hickory-smoked Hashed Browns • Romaine Salad with Tomatoes and Parmesan

Serves 4

The ultimate among steaks, fillets cut from the tenderloin, combined with a skillet of smoke-infused hashed browns and a summer salad embellished with shaved Parmesan cheese. Serve with your finest Cabernet Sauvignon.

Fillet Steaks with Red Wine

Four 6-ounce fillet steaks, each about
  1½ inches thick
4 shallots
2 garlic cloves
¼ cup olive oil
2 cups dry red wine
Salt and freshly ground white pepper
  to taste
4 fresh thyme sprigs, plus some for
  garnish

Prepare a charcoal fire in a grill. Place the fillets in a nonaluminum bowl and add all the remaining ingredients except the garnish. Let sit at room temperature, turning once, while the coals are heating.

When the coals are hot, drain the steaks, reserving the marinade, and sear them for 2 minutes on each side. Baste the steaks with the marinade, cover the grill, partially open the vents, and cook for 3 to 4 minutes on each side, for a total cooking time of 7 to 8 minutes for medium rare.

Remove the steaks from the grill to a serving plate and cover them loosely with aluminum foil. Let sit for 10 minutes. Meanwhile, pour the leftover marinade into a saucepan and cook over medium-high heat for about 5 minutes, or until the liquid is slightly reduced and thickened. Discard the thyme sprigs. Pool a little sauce on each serving plate and place the steak on top of the sauce, garnished with thyme sprigs. Serve the remaining sauce separately.

Hickory-smoked Hashed Browns

¼ cup hickory chips
1 pound unpeeled boiling potatoes, scrubbed and cut into ¼-inch dice
1 red bell pepper, cored, seeded, and cut into ¼-inch dice
1 yellow bell pepper, cored, seeded, and cut into ¼-inch dice
1 red onion, cut into ¼-inch dice
2 tablespoons olive oil
Salt and freshly ground white pepper to taste
¼ cup minced fresh flat-leaf parsley

Place the hickory chips in water to cover for 30 minutes. In a medium bowl, combine the potatoes, peppers, onion, 1 tablespoon of the oil, salt, and pepper; stir to mix. Heat a large cast-iron skillet on a charcoal grill over medium-hot coals and coat it with the remaining tablespoon of olive oil. Add the potato mixture, cover the grill, and cook for 15 minutes, stirring every 5 minutes. Drain the hickory chips and sprinkle them over the coals; cover the grill and cook another 5 minutes, for a total cooking time of 20 minutes. Remove from the grill and cover to keep warm if not serving immediately. Just before serving, stir in the parsley.

Romaine Salad with Tomatoes and Parmesan

4 slices French bread
8 tablespoons olive oil
1 garlic clove, halved
1 head romaine lettuce
2 tablespoons fresh lemon juice
½ teaspoon Worcestershire sauce
Salt and freshly ground white pepper to taste
4 tomatoes, cut into wedges, or 1½ cups stemmed cherry tomatoes
1 small piece (about 1 ounce) Parmesan cheese

Dizzle the bread slices on both sides with 2 tablespoons of the olive oil and toast them on the grill. Rub with the cut garlic and cut into large croutons.

Tear the romaine leaves into bite-sized pieces and place them in a glass, ceramic, or wooden bowl. In a small bowl, whisk together the remaining 6 tablespoons olive oil, lemon juice, Worcestershire, salt, and pepper. Pour over the lettuce, tossing to coat the leaves well. Add the tomatoes and toss gently. Correct the seasoning. Using a potato peeler, cut thin shavings of the Parmesan, about ¼ cup. Sprinkle the Parmesan and croutons over the salad.

North Country Grill-roasted Duck

Wild Rice Pancakes • Grilled Radicchio and Endive Salad

Serves 4

Duck is a natural for the grill: The layer of fat under its skin acts as a built-in baste, and its assertive flavor is complemented by the fragrance of charcoal and wood smoke. Savory pancakes made with wild rice are the perfect side dish. The slightly bitter tastes of grilled radicchio and endive, dressed in a mustardy vinaigrette, round out this north country menu. If you want a vegetable, try grilled green onions. Côte du Rhône or Pinot Noir goes well with duck.

1 cup alder wood chips (optional)
One 4-pound duck
Salt and freshly ground white pepper
   to taste
1 leek with some of the green leaves, cut
   into large pieces
1 apple, cut into quarters
1 handful fresh flat-leaf parsley, plus
   1 tablespoon minced parsley

½ yellow onion, chopped
6 garlic cloves, crushed, plus 6 garlic
   cloves cut into thin slices
3 cups dry red wine

Prepare an indirect charcoal fire in a grill and place a 9-by-13-inch drip pan in the center of the fuel grate. Place the optional wood chips in water to cover. Rinse the duck inside and out and pat dry with paper towels. Sprinkle the inside of the cavity with salt and pepper. Put the leek, apple, the handful of parsley, onion, and crushed garlic cloves inside the duck. Twist the wings back under the duck and truss with a cotton string to tie the drumsticks together and close the body and neck cavities. Place the duck in a shallow nonaluminum pan. Combine the red wine, minced parsley, and sliced garlic, and pour the mixture over the duck; let sit at room temperature until the coals are ready.

When the coals are medium-hot, drain the optional wood chips and sprinkle half of them over the coals. Remove the duck from the marinade, place it breast-side up in the center of the cooking rack, and grill for 1 hour, basting with the marinade every 15 minutes. After 1 hour, rebuild the fire with new coals. Sprinkle the remaining wood chips over the coals. Cook the duck another 30 minutes, basting it after 15 minutes, or until the breast meat registers 160°F on an instant-read thermometer, for a total cooking time of about 1½ hours. At this point, when the thigh is pierced with a knife, the juices should still have a trace of pink.

Transfer the duck from the grill to a grooved carving board and cover it loosely with aluminum foil; let sit for 15 minutes. Remove the foil, carve the duck, and serve with the carving juices poured over it.

Wild Rice Pancakes

1 cup wild rice
2½ cups salted water
3 eggs
¼ cup milk
½ cup unbleached all-purpose flour
½ cup shredded Gruyère cheese
¼ cup finely shredded Parmesan cheese
2 large shallots, minced
¼ cup minced fresh flat-leaf parsley
½ teaspoon salt, or to taste
¼ teaspoon freshly ground white
**   pepper, or to taste**
2 teaspoons butter
2 teaspoons canola oil
Fresh flat-leaf parsley sprigs for garnish

Wash the wild rice in cold water; drain. Place the salted water in a medium saucepan, add the wild rice, partially cover, and cook for 40 to 50 minutes, or until the rice is tender. Drain off any excess water and set aside.

In a medium bowl, beat together the eggs and milk. Stir in the flour until blended, then stir in the cooked rice, cheeses, shallots, parsley, salt, and pepper.

In a large cast-iron skillet over medium heat, melt 1 teaspoon butter with 1 teaspoon oil. When the butter bubbles, add 3 or 4 large spoonfuls of pancake batter to the pan, pressing down on each pancake with a metal spatula to flatten it. Cook the pancakes for 3 to 5 minutes on each side, or until golden brown. Place the pancakes on a plate in an oven set on very low heat and repeat to cook all the pancakes, adding the remaining butter and oil as necessary. Serve warm, garnished with parsley sprigs.

Grilled Radicchio and Endive Salad

1 head radicchio
1 head endive
6 tablespoons extra-virgin olive oil
3 tablespoons balsamic vinegar
5 cups mixed baby lettuce leaves
1 teaspoon Dijon mustard
1 garlic clove, minced
Salt and freshly ground white pepper
**   to taste**
Fresh lemon juice to taste (optional)

Separate the radicchio and endive leaves and place them in a salad bowl. In a small bowl, combine 2 tablespoons of the olive oil and 2 tablespoons of the balsamic vinegar. Using your hands, coat the radicchio and endive leaves evenly with this mixture. Place the leaves in an oiled grill basket or on an oiled grilling rack and sear them for 1 or 2 minutes on each side over medium coals; they should be slightly wilted and lightly charred. Transfer them from the grill to the salad bowl.

Add the baby lettuce leaves to the salad bowl. In a small bowl, combine the remaining 4 tablespoons oil and 1 tablespoon balsamic vinegar with the mustard, garlic, salt, and pepper. Pour this mixture over the greens and grilled leaves and toss. Adjust the seasoning, adding a few drops of lemon juice if you like.

GRILLED ROCKY MOUNTAIN TROUT

Fresh-Corn Cakes • Marinated Cucumber and Red Onion Salad

Serves 4

The perfume of charcoal is the ideal flavor-enhancer for the sweet white flesh of rainbow trout, here served with hot pancakes made with fresh corn, and a salad of red onion and cucumber slices wilted in a mild marinade. If you want to add a side dish, try the Green Rice Casserole on page 32. Either a French Colombard or a Johannisberg Riesling is nice with this menu.

Grilled Rocky Mountain Trout

4 fresh rainbow trout
2 tablespoons olive oil
Salt and freshly ground white pepper
**   to taste**
4 green onions, chopped
2 tablespoons minced fresh sage
4 garlic cloves, minced
Fresh sage sprigs for garnish

Light a charcoal fire in a grill. Wash the trout inside and out and pat dry with paper towels. Coat the trout evenly inside and out with olive oil, and sprinkle them inside and out with salt and pepper. In a small bowl, combine all of the remaining ingredients, except for the garnish, and sprinkle them evenly inside the fish. Let the fish sit at room temperature until the fire is ready.

When the coals are hot, clean the grill with a grill brush if necessary and oil it with a brush or vegetable-oil spray. Place the trout on the cooking rack and grill for 5 minutes on each side (for a total cooking time of 10 minutes), or until the flesh is opaque throughout. Remove the trout from the grill and serve on heated plates, garnished with sage sprigs.

Fresh-Corn Cakes

1 cup unbleached all-purpose flour
2 teaspoons baking powder
1 teaspoon baking soda
1 teaspoon salt
1½ cups buttermilk
2 tablespoons butter, melted, plus 2
　　teaspoons unmelted butter
1 cup fresh corn kernels
Freshly ground white pepper to taste
2 teaspoons canola oil

In a medium bowl, stir together the flour, baking powder, baking soda, and salt. In a small bowl, combine the buttermilk and the 2 tablespoons melted butter. Pour the liquid mixture into the dry mixture and stir until just smooth. Stir in the corn kernels and the pepper.

　　In a large cast-iron skillet over medium heat, melt 1 teaspoon of the unmelted butter with 1 teaspoon of oil. When the butter bubbles, make 3 or 4 corn cakes at a time by pouring ¼ cup batter per cake into the skillet. When the surface of each corn cake is completely covered with bubbles (about 4 or 5 minutes), turn it to brown the other side. If necessary, turn again to brown both sides as you like. Place the cakes on a plate in a very low oven and repeat to use all the batter, adding the remaining butter and oil as needed. Serve warm.

Marinated Cucumber and Red Onion Salad

1 unpeeled English cucumber, or
　　3 regular cucumbers, peeled
1 small red onion
½ cup distilled white vinegar
2 tablespoons water
2 teaspoons sugar
1 teaspoon salt
1 tablespoon minced fresh dill weed, or
　　more to taste
8 large lettuce leaves

Cut the cucumber and red onion into paper-thin slices and place them in a medium glass or ceramic bowl. Stir in the vinegar, water, sugar, and salt. Cover and chill for 2 hours. Drain off all but about ¼ cup of the liquid; stir in the dill weed. Place 2 lettuce leaves on each of 4 chilled salad plates and divide the salad on top of the leaves.

Grill-roasted Rib Roast

Scalloped Potatoes • Butter Lettuce Salad with Honey-Mustard Vinaigrette

Serves 6 to 8

Here a luxurious cut of beef—the standing rib—is grilled whole and served with everybody's favorite, scalloped potatoes, and a green salad with a tangy dressing. Serve your favorite red wine alongside.

Grill-roasted Rib Roast

5 to 6 garlic cloves, cut into slivers
One 6½-pound standing rib roast with chine bone removed, trimmed of rib ends and all but ¼ inch fat
Olive oil for coating
Salt and paprika to taste
½ cup dry white wine or vermouth
1 cup canned low-salt beef broth (optional)

Prepare an indirect charcoal fire in a grill and place a 9-by-13-inch drip pan in the center of the coals. Insert the garlic slivers between the layer of fat and the meat.

Rub the olive oil evenly all over the meat, and sprinkle the meat on all sides with salt and paprika. Let stand at room temperature until the coals are ready.

When the coals are hot, add 1 inch of water to the drip pan. Sear the roast directly over the coals for 3 to 4 minutes on all 4 sides. Place the roast fat-side up over the drip pan, cover the grill, partially open the vents, and cook for 1 hour. (An in-grill thermometer should maintain a heat of 350°F.)

Rebuild the fire by adding more coals. Add more water to the drip pan if necessary. Cook the roast another 30 minutes to 1 hour for medium rare, or until an instant-read thermometer inserted in the center of the roast registers 130°F. Remove the roast to a carving board and cover it loosely with aluminum foil; let sit for 10 minutes. Meanwhile, pour the juices from the drip pan into a large

measuring cup; pour off as much fat as possible. Pour the drippings into a saucepan. Add the white wine or vermouth and the optional broth (if you need more liquid) and boil to reduce the liquid slightly. Uncover and slice the beef; serve the sauce alongside.

Scalloped Potatoes

1 garlic clove, halved
2 cups half-and-half
2 tablespoons butter
2½ pounds boiling potatoes, peeled and cut into thin slices
Salt and freshly ground white pepper to taste
½ cup shredded Gruyère cheese
½ cup finely shredded Parmesan cheese
Milk as needed to cover potatoes

Preheat the oven to 300°F. Place the garlic in a medium saucepan and add the half-and-half. Bring the half-and-half to a simmer over low heat.

Meanwhile, use 1 tablespoon of the butter to coat the inside of a gratin dish about 12 inches in diameter and 2 inches deep. Layer half of the sliced potatoes in the dish and sprinkle them with salt, pepper, and half of the shredded cheeses.

Layer the remaining half of the potatoes in the dish and sprinkle again with salt, pepper, and the remaining cheese. Pour the hot half-and-half over the potatoes. Add milk as necessary to come up to the final cheese layer. Dot the top with the remaining 1 tablespoon butter. Place the gratin dish in the oven and cook for 1 to 1¼ hours, or until the potatoes are tender and golden brown. Serve warm.

Butter Lettuce with Honey-Mustard Vinaigrette

4 heads butter lettuce
8 shallots, cut into thin slices
½ cup olive oil
3 tablespoons red wine vinegar
2 teaspoons honey
3 teaspoons Dijon mustard
Salt and freshly ground white pepper to taste

Place the butter lettuce leaves in a salad bowl and sprinkle the shallots over them. In a small bowl, combine all the remaining ingredients and whisk until emulsified. Pour the vinaigrette over the lettuce and shallots, and toss. Adjust the seasoning and serve.

SOUTHWESTERN PORK LOIN WITH SALSA VERDE

Corn Pudding • Garlic Sopaipillas

Serves 6

The flavors of the American Southwest reflect its Native American, Anglo, Spanish, and Mexican influences. Our Southwestern menu features grilled stuffed pork loin slices served with a cooked tomatillo sauce, a souffléd casserole of fresh corn, and the fried puffed bread of New Mexico, sopaipillas ("sofa pillows"), with a whiff of garlic. Grilled zucchini would go well with this menu. Serve with chilled Mexican beer.

Southwestern Pork Loin with Salsa Verde

1 cup mesquite wood chips
2 poblano chilies

SALSA VERDE

1½ pounds fresh tomatillos, husked, or two 12-ounce cans tomatillos, drained
1 tablespoon olive oil

4 garlic cloves, minced
1 small onion, finely chopped
1 jalapeño, minced (remove the seeds first if you prefer a mild sauce)
½ cup minced fresh cilantro
1 cup canned low-salt chicken broth
½ teaspoon salt
Pinch of sugar

One 3-pound boneless pork loin
¼ cup olive oil
1 teaspoon ground cumin
3 garlic cloves, minced
Salt to taste
Fresh cilantro sprigs for garnish

Light a charcoal fire in a grill and place the mesquite wood chips in water to cover. When the coals are flaming, sear the chilies over the fire until they are blackened on all sides. Place the chilies in a paper bag, close it, and let sit for 15 minutes. While the chilies are cooling, start the salsa verde: If using fresh tomatillos, place them in a large saucepan, cover them with salted water, and bring to a boil. Reduce heat, cover, and simmer for 10 minutes, or until tender; drain. Place the cooked or drained canned tomatillos in a blender or food processor and blend to a coarse puree. In a large skillet, heat the olive oil over medium-low heat and cook the garlic and onion for about 3 minutes, or until translucent. Stir in the pureed tomatillos and all the remaining salsa ingredients. Simmer the salsa, uncovered, for about 20 minutes, or until it is thickened and the flavors have developed; adjust the seasoning and keep warm.

While the salsa is cooking, place the pork loin on a cutting board and open it out flat. In a small bowl, combine the oil, cumin, garlic, and salt. Rub half of this mixture evenly over the inside of the pork. Rub the blackened skin off the chilies and cut the chilies into narrow strips. Place the chili strips evenly over the pork. Roll the pork closed. Beginning about ¾ inch from one end, tie the pork closed at 1½-inch intervals with cotton string; there should be 6 ties. Using a large slicing knife, cut

the pork into 6 crosswise slices about 1½ inches thick; rub with remaining oil mixture and let sit at room temperature until the coals are ready.

When the coals are hot, sear the pork rolls for 3 minutes on each side. Drain the wood chips and sprinkle them over the coals. Turn the pork rolls, cover the grill, partially close the vents, and cook the rolls 4 to 6 minutes on each side, for a total cooking time of 14 to 18 minutes. Transfer the rolls to a platter and serve them in a pool of salsa verde, garnished with cilantro sprigs; pass the extra sauce separately.

Corn Pudding

6 ears corn
1 tablespoon butter
1 tablespoon flour
1 cup milk
3 eggs, separated
1 teaspoon salt
¼ teaspoon cayenne pepper
¼ cup plus 2 tablespoons finely shredded Parmesan cheese

Preheat the oven to 350°F and butter an 8-cup casserole. Cut the kernels from the

ears of corn and scrape the milk from the cobs. In a large saucepan, melt the butter over medium-low heat; stir in the flour and cook, stirring, for 2 to 3 minutes. Whisk in the milk and simmer, stirring occasionally, until slightly thickened, 10 to 15 minutes. Beat a large spoonful of this sauce into the egg yolks, then whisk the yolks into the sauce; whisk over medium-low heat for about 5 minutes. Blend in the corn kernels and their milk, salt, and cayenne.

In a large bowl, beat the egg whites until soft peaks form. Stir a large spoonful of the whites into the corn mixture, then fold in the remaining whites. Fold in ¼ cup of the Parmesan. Pour the batter into the prepared dish, sprinkle the remaining Parmesan on top, and bake for about 40 minutes, or until golden brown and set. Serve warm.

Garlic Sopaipillas

1½ cups unbleached all-purpose flour
¾ teaspoon salt
Pinch of cayenne pepper
2 teaspoons baking powder
1 garlic clove, minced
2 tablespoons shortening
½ cup warm water

Corn or canola oil for deep-frying
Butter for serving

In a medium bowl, stir together the flour, salt, cayenne, baking powder, and garlic. Add the shortening and cut it in with a pastry cutter or your fingers until the mixture is the texture of coarse meal. Pour in the warm water all at once and stir until the mixture forms a ball. On a lightly floured surface, knead the dough for 4 or 5 minutes, or until smooth and elastic. Cover it with a clean cotton towel and let sit for 15 minutes.

Into a large, heavy kettle or deep-fryer, pour the oil to a depth of 3 inches. Heat over medium-high heat to a temperature of 400°F. While the oil is heating, divide the dough in half and roll out each half into a circle ⅛ inch thick. Cut each circle into 4 wedges. When the oil is hot, deep-fry 2 or 3 pieces of dough for about 3 minutes, turning them as necessary to cook all sides. When the sopaipillas are evenly golden brown and puffed, use a slotted spoon to transfer them to a plate lined with paper towels for draining, and place the plate in a very low oven. Repeat until all the sopaipillas are cooked. Serve warm, with butter.

GRILL-ROASTED HAM, SOUTHERN STYLE

Black-eyed Pea Salad • Hickory-smoked Okra

Makes 12 to 14 servings

Ham is always a great main course for a party, and long, slow cooking in a charcoal grill with hickory smoke is one of the best ways to cook ham—it comes out moist and tender, with all the perfume of the grill. The Southern theme of our menu is continued with a salad of marinated black-eyed peas and a side dish of hickory-smoked grilled okra. Serve iced tea, beer, a dry rosé, or Gewürztraminer to drink.

Grill-roasted Ham, Southern Style

3 cups hickory chips
One 10- to 12-pound partially cooked
  bone-in butt-end half ham
2 bottles beer, or 4 cups apple juice, dry
  white wine, or water, plus a little extra
  liquid to thin the sauce, if you like
Whole cloves for garnish

BROWN SUGAR AND MUSTARD GLAZE

1 cup packed brown sugar
½ cup Dijon mustard
2 teaspoons ground cumin
⅛ to ¼ teaspoon ground cinnamon,
  or to taste
⅛ to ¼ teaspoon cayenne pepper, or
  to taste

Light an indirect charcoal fire in a grill and place a 9-by-13-inch metal drip pan in the center of the fuel grate. Place the hickory chips in water to cover. Remove the ham from the refrigerator.

When the coals are medium-hot, pour the beer, apple juice, wine, or water into the drip pan. Drain the hickory chips and sprinkle about one third of them over the coals. Place the ham on the cooking rack over the drip pan, cover the grill, partially close the top and bottom vents, and grill the ham for 1 hour. If you have an in-grill thermometer, the heat should stay at around 350°F. If the fire is not hot enough, open the vents fully or remove the lid and stir the coals. After 1 hour, rebuild the fire by adding more coals, and sprinkle another third of the hickory chips over the coals. Cook the ham for 1 more hour.

After the second hour, carefully remove the ham from the grill to a carving board, using 2 large forks inserted into opposite ends of the ham. Rebuild the fire by adding new coals. With a sharp knife, cut off and discard all the skin and all but ¼ inch of the fat from the ham. Score the fat into diamonds by making diagonal cuts about 1½ inches apart in opposite directions; cut down to, but not into, the meat. Insert a whole clove in the corner of each diagonal.

To make the glaze: In a small bowl, stir together all the ingredients until smooth and liquified. Brush or spoon the mixture evenly over the outside of the ham. Sprinkle the remaining hickory chips over the coals. Place the ham on the cooking rack, cover, and grill for about 1 more

hour, basting the ham with the sugar-mustard mixture every 10 or 15 minutes, for a total cooking time of about 3 hours.

When the ham is golden brown and glazed all over and the internal temperature near the center (but not touching the bone) is 130°F, carefully remove it to the carving board, again using 2 forks. Cover the ham loosely with aluminum foil and let sit for 15 minutes.

Cut the ham into thin slices. Pour off any juices from the carving board into the sugar-mustard mixture; add a little beer, apple juice, or white wine to make a thin sauce. Pour a spoonful of sauce over each serving and pass the remaining sauce at the table.

Black-eyed Pea Salad

3 cups (21 ounces) dried black-eyed peas
6 garlic cloves, crushed
2 yellow onions, chopped
2 whole small dried red peppers
2 bay leaves
2 teaspoons crumbled dried thyme
¾ cup olive oil
½ cup red wine vinegar

2 red and 2 yellow (or 4 red) bell
  peppers, cored, seeded, and chopped
4 cups red or mixed red and yellow
  cherry tomatoes, stemmed and halved
2 red onions, chopped
½ cup minced fresh cilantro
Tabasco sauce and salt to taste

Pick over the black-eyed peas and remove
any stones. Place the black-eyed peas in a
large saucepan and add the garlic, onions,
dried peppers, bay leaves, thyme, and
water to cover. Cover the pan and simmer
for 45 minutes to 1 hour, or until the peas
are just tender but not falling apart. Drain
the peas in a colander and place them in a
large ceramic or stainless steel bowl. Pour
the oil and vinegar over the peas and stir
to coat them. Let the peas sit until cooled
to room temperature. Stir in the remaining
ingredients and serve at room temperature.

Hickory-smoked Okra

¼ cup hickory chips
3 pounds large okra
Olive oil for coating
Kosher salt for sprinkling

Place the hickory chips in water to cover
for 30 minutes. Place the okra in a large
cast-iron pan or in a grill basket and coat
them evenly with olive oil. Place the pan
or grill basket on the cooking rack and
grill over hot coals for 3 to 4 minutes. Stir
and cook another 2 minutes. Drain the
hickory chips and sprinkle them over the
coals. Cover the grill and cook the okra
for 3 minutes. Sprinkle with kosher salt
and serve hot.

WINE COUNTRY LEG OF LAMB WITH GARLIC-SAGE BUTTER

Fresh Fig and Goat Cheese Salad • Grilled Sourdough Bread with Tomatoes and Basil

Serves 8

Northern California is the home of some of the best food in the United States, as our Napa Valley–inspired menu shows. Butterflied leg of lamb grills beautifully and is a perfect choice for entertaining, especially when paired with a smooth butter flavored with garlic and fresh sage. The fig and goat cheese salad and the grilled sourdough bread with a topping of fresh tomatoes and basil reflect the Mediterranean influences of this regional cuisine. If you want to add a vegetable, try grilled summer squash or Japanese eggplant. Choose either a Northern California Merlot or a Zinfandel to drink.

Wine Country Leg of Lamb with Garlic-Sage Butter

1 large handful vine cuttings
One 4-pound butterflied leg of lamb
4 garlic cloves

¼ cup olive oil
2 tablespoons minced fresh thyme
2 tablespoons minced fresh oregano
½ cup Madeira or dry sherry
½ cup dry white wine
Grape clusters and fresh thyme and oregano sprigs for garnish

Light a charcoal fire in a grill and place the vine cuttings in water to cover. Place the leg of lamb in a shallow nonaluminum pan. In a small bowl, mix together all the remaining ingredients except the garnishes. Pour this mixture over the lamb and let it sit at room temperature until the fire is ready, turning the lamb once after about 20 minutes.

When the coals are hot, place the lamb on the cooking rack and sear it for 3 minutes on each side. Cover the grill and cook the lamb for 12 minutes on each side (for a total cooking time of 30 minutes),

basting it before turning, or until an instant-read thermometer inserted in the thickest part of the lamb reads 150°F. (At this point the thick part will be medium rare and the thinner parts medium.) Transfer the lamb from the grill to a carving board, cover it loosely with aluminum foil, and let sit for 10 minutes. Meanwhile, pour the remaining marinade into a small saucepan and boil it for several minutes until it is reduced by about half. Carve the lamb and pour the carving juices into the sauce. Garnish and serve; pass the sauce separately.

Fresh Fig and Goat Cheese Salad

8 cups mixed baby lettuce leaves
16 small fresh figs, halved
½ cup fresh mild white goat cheese, crumbled
½ cup extra-virgin olive oil
1 tablespoon red wine vinegar
1 tablespoon balsamic vinegar
Salt and freshly ground white pepper to taste

In a salad bowl, combine the lettuce, figs, and goat cheese. In a small bowl, combine the remaining ingredients and toss with the salad ingredients; serve at once.

Grilled Sourdough Bread with Tomatoes and Basil

1½ baskets cherry tomatoes, stemmed and coarsely chopped
¼ cup minced fresh basil
2 tablespoons extra-virgin olive oil, plus more for drizzling
Salt and freshly ground white pepper to taste
Eight 1-inch-thick slices sourdough bread (sandwich size)
2 large garlic cloves, halved

In a medium bowl, combine the tomatoes, basil, 2 tablespoons of the olive oil, salt, and pepper; set aside. Drizzle the bread on both sides with olive oil. Place the bread over a medium-hot fire and toast for 2 minutes on each side, or until lightly browned. Rub the cut half of a garlic clove on both sides of each toast. Top the toasts with the tomato-basil mixture and serve hot.

MAIL-ORDER SOURCES

GRILLS

Hasty Bake
7656 E. 46th Street
Tulsa, OK 74145
800-426-6836
918-665-8225
Charcoal ovens

Kamado
BSW, Inc.
4680 East Second Street
Benicia, CA 94510
707-745-8175;
fax 707-745-9708
Ceramic grill-ovens in
several sizes.

Weber
Weber-Stephen Products
Company
560 Hicks Road
Palatine, IL 60067-6971
847-705-8660 (in Illinois),
or 800-446-1071;
fax 847-705-7971
web site
www.webberbbq.com
Charcoal kettle grills
in several sizes and styles.

CHARCOAL AND SMOKING WOODS

Charcoal Companion
7955 Edgewater Drive
Oakland, CA 94621
510-632-2100 (in California),
or 800-521-0505;
fax 510-632-1986
A wide variety of smoking
woods.

Desert Mesquite of Arizona
3458 East Illini Street
Phoenix, AZ 85040
602-437-3135
Mesquite smoking wood.

Hasty Bake
7656 E. 46th Street
Tulsa, OK 74145
800-426-6836
918-665-8225
Oak and Hickory lump
charcoal

Humphrey Charcoal Corporation
P.O. Box 440
Brookville, PA 15825
814-849-2302

Hardwood charcoal;
wholesale and regional only.

Lazzari Fuel Company
P.O. Box 34051
San Francisco, CA 94134
415-467-2970 (in California),
or 800-242-7265;
fax 415-468-2298
Mesquite charcoal and
smoking woods.

Luhr Jensen & Sons, Inc.
P.O. Box 297
Hood River, OR 97031
541-386-3811 (in Oregon),
or 800-535-1711;
fax 541-386-4917
web site
www.luhr-jensen.com
Smoking woods.

GRILLING ACCESSORIES

Charcoal Companion
7955 Edgewater Drive
Oakland, CA 94621
510-632-2100 (in California),
or 800-521-0505;
fax 510-632-1986
A wide variety of grill
accessories.

FOODS

Brae Beef
P.O. Box 1561
Greenwich, CT 06836-1561
203-869-0106;
fax 203-661-2689
Naturally raised beef.

D'Artagnan
280 Wilson Avenue
Newark, NJ 07105
800-327-8246;
fax 973-465-1870
web site
www.dartagnan.com
Naturally raised chicken;
farm-raised game birds, game
meats, and lamb.

Durham–Night Bird
358 Shaw Road, No. A
South San Francisco, CA
94080
415-737-5873;
fax 415-737-5880
Naturally raised chicken,
game birds, beef, and free-
range veal.

Pacific Seafoods
3380 Southeast Powell Blvd.
Portland, OR 97202
503-233-4891;
fax 503-234-9242
Northwest Pacific salmon
and other fresh fish and
shellfish in season.

Simply Shrimp
7794 NW 44th Street
Ft. Lauderdale, FL 33351
800-833-0888;
fax 954-741-6127
Gulf shrimp and a wide
variety of other fresh fish and
shellfish in season.

Summerfield Farms
10044 James Monroe
Highway
Culpepper, VA 22701
540-547-9600;
fax 540-547-9628
Naturally raised veal, lamb,
and poultry.

Walnut Acres
Penns Creek, PA 17862
800-433-3998,
fax: 717-837-1146
web site
www.walnutacres.com
A wide variety of organic
foods, including naturally
raised chicken, meats, and
turkey; grains; dried fruits;
cheeses; fresh fruits and
vegetables. Catalogue;
24-hour mail order.

Wolfe's Neck Farm
10 Burnett Road
Freeport, ME 04032
207-865-4469;
fax 207-865-6927
Naturally raised beef; regional
home delivery; retail store.

Index

A
alder wood chips, 18
  with duck, 47–48
  with salmon, 37–38
apple wood chips, 18

B
balsamic vinegar, 18
barbecued
  chicken, Memphis, 41–42
  ribs, Texas, 29–30
basil, 16
  butter, 37–38
  and tomatoes with grilled
    sourdough bread, 67
basting brush, long-handled,
  25
beef
  fillet steaks with red wine,
    45
  grill-roasted rib roast, 54
  Texas barbecued ribs,
    29–30
bent-blade spatula, long-handled, 25
black-eyed pea salad, 62–64
bread
  garlic sopaipillas, 60
  grilled sourdough bread
    with tomatoes and basil,
    67
  skillet corn bread with
    green chilies, 30
briquettes, charcoal, 19
brown sugar and mustard
  glaze, 61–62
butter
  basil, 37–38
  garlic-sage, 65–67
  lettuce with honey-mus-
    tard vinaigrette, 56
buttermilk, 15

C
Cajun shrimp, 34
canola oil, 16
charcoal
  briquettes, 19, 21
  chimney, 21
  hardwood, 19–21
  lighter, 21
  mesquite, 19–21
  quantity of, 22
  rails, 22
cheese(s), 15
  fresh fig and goat cheese
    salad, 67
  romaine salad with
    Oregon blue cheese, 38
  romaine salad with toma-
    toes and Parmesan, 46
chicken, Memphis barbe-
  cued, 41–42
chilies, 15
  green, skillet corn bread
    with, 30
chimney, charcoal, 21
coleslaw, red and green 30
cooking rack, cleaning, 19
corn, 15–16
  bread with green chilies,
    skillet, 30
  cakes, fresh, 52
  oil, 16
  on the cob, grilled, 38
  pudding, 58–60
cucumber and red onion
    salad, marinated, 52

D
direct fire, 21
distilled white vinegar, 18
doneness, judging, 23
drip pan, 22

duck, north country grill-
  roasted, 47–48

E
endive salad, grillled radicchio and, 50

F
fig and goat cheese salad,
  fresh, 67
fillet steaks with red wine, 45
fire
  judging heat of, 22
  lighting, 21
  rebuilding, 23
  regulating, 22-23
fish, *see* salmon, trout
flare-ups, 23, 25
flat-leaf parsley, 16

G
garlic
  -sage butter, 65–67
  sopaipillas, 60
goat cheese and fresh fig
    salad, 67
green chilies, canned peeled,
  15
  in skillet corn bread, 30
grill
  baskets, 25
  brush, wire, 19, 25
  cleaning, 19
  mitts, 25
grilling grids, 25

H
ham, grill-roasted, Southern
  style, 61–62
hardwood charcoal, 19
hashed browns, hickory-
  smoked, 46

herbs, 16
hickory
  -smoked hash browns, 46
  -smoked okra, 64
  -smoked tomatoes, 36
  wood chips, 18
honey-mustard vinaigrette, 56

I
indirect fire, 21–22

J
jalapeño chilies, 15

L
lamb, leg of, with garlic-sage
  butter, 65–67
lighter, charcoal, 21

M
meats, 16; *see also* beef, pork,
  ham, lamb
Memphis barbecued chicken,
  41–42
mesquite
  charcoal, 19–21
  wood chips, 18
Midwest potato salad, 42–43
mustard
  and brown sugar glaze,
    61–62
  -honey vinaigrette, 56

N
north country grill-roasted
  duck, 47–48
Northwest salmon with basil
  butter, 37–38

O
oils, 16
okra, hickory-smoked, 64